ATOMS

IT MATTERS

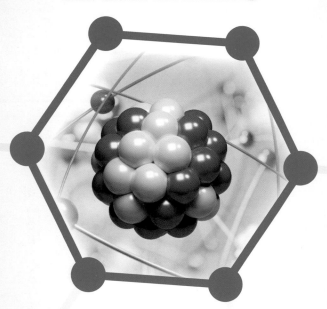

BARBARA MARTINA LINDE

PowerKiDS press™

NEW YORK

Published in 2020 by The Rosen Publishing Group, Inc.
29 East 21st Street, New York, NY 10010

Editor: Elizabeth Krajnik
Book Design: Michael Flynn
Acknowledgement: Subject Matter Expert, Jeffrey A. Hinkley, PhD.

Photo Credits: Cover, p. 1 vchal/Shutterstock.com; (series molecular background) pro500/Shutterstock.com; p. 4 valdis torms/Shutterstock.com; p. 5 Luciano Mortula/Shutterstock.com; p. 6 Everett - Art/Shutterstock.com; p. 7 Photo 12/Universal Images Group/Getty Images; p. 9 https://commons.wikimedia.org/wiki/File:Dalton_ John_desk.jpg; p. 10 Alex Andrei/Shutterstock.com; p. 11 Pavel Sapozhnikov/Shutterstock.com; p. 12 Prachaya Roekdeethaweesab/Shutterstock.com; p. 13 (left and right) yaruna/Shutterstock.com; p. 14 Emmily/Shutterstock.com; p. 15 Alejo Miranda/Shutterstock.com; pp. 17, 24 Science & Society Picture Library/SSPL/Getty Images; p. 18 ND700/ Shutterstock.com; p. 19 https://commons.wikimedia.org/wiki/File:Chlorophyll_spacefilling_model.jpg; p. 21 (top) KaliAntye/Shutterstock.com; p. 21 (bottom) Tyler Olson/Shutterstock.com; p. 23 lazyllama/Shutterstock.com; p. 25 geogif/Shutterstock.com; p. 27 Rabbitmindphoto/Shutterstock.com; p. 29 https://en.wikipedia.org/wiki/Particle_ accelerator#/media/File:Fermilab.jpg; p. 30 Syda Productions/Shutterstock.com.

Library of Congress Cataloging-in-Publication Data

Names: Linde, Barbara M., author.
Title: Atoms : it matters / Barbara Martina Linde.
Description: New York : PowerKids Press, [2020] | Series: Spotlight on
  physical science | Includes index.
Identifiers: LCCN 2019017449| ISBN 9781725312890 (pbk.) | ISBN 9781725312920
  (library bound) | ISBN 9781725312906 (6 pack)
Subjects: LCSH: Atoms--Juvenile literature. | Atomic theory--Juvenile
  literature. | Matter--Properties--Juvenile literature.
Classification: LCC QC173.16 .L56 2020 | DDC 539.7--dc23
LC record available at https://lccn.loc.gov/2019017449

Manufactured in the United States of America

CPSIA Compliance Information: Batch #CWPK20. For further information contact Rosen Publishing, New York, New York at 1-800-237-9932.

CONTENTS

CHAPTER ONE

AMAZING ATOMS

What is the world made of? All matter on Earth is made up of atoms! An atom is the smallest particle of an element that can exist. Atoms can't be seen with the naked eye. They can't be seen with a regular microscope either. However, electron microscopes can help us see individual atoms. Different kinds of atoms are different sizes and weights. Some kinds of atoms, such as hydrogen atoms, are abundant, while others are much more rare.

How do we know about atoms? It's taken a long time and a lot of imagination and hard work to learn about them. The ancient Greeks first came up with the idea of atoms. Early scientists continued studying them. Today, scientists are learning even more about these amazing building blocks of matter.

Everything in this picture is made of atoms.

CHAPTER TWO

ATOMISM

Thousands of years ago, Greek **philosophers** wondered about the objects around them. What were things made of? What was the smallest part of something? They imagined that everything was made of tiny particles of different shapes and sizes. These particles were too small to see. The philosopher Democritus called these particles *atomos*, which means "uncuttable." The Greeks' ideas about them were called atomism.

DEMOCRITUS

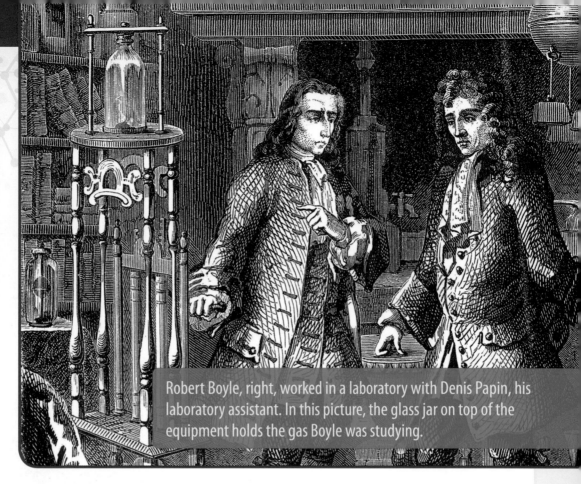

Robert Boyle, right, worked in a laboratory with Denis Papin, his laboratory assistant. In this picture, the glass jar on top of the equipment holds the gas Boyle was studying.

In the 1600s, scientists in Europe knew about Greek atomism. Like the Greeks, they thought a lot about the everyday world. However, they looked at things in a more scientific way. Robert Boyle did experiments and showed that air might be made up of fast-moving particles. He called these particles "atomes." Sir Isaac Newton showed more about how air pressure might work. Still, he couldn't prove that gas was made up of particles. Newton challenged other scientists to keep experimenting.

CHAPTER THREE

JOHN DALTON

Scientists kept studying the idea of atoms. In the early 1800s, English **chemist** John Dalton took huge steps, developing his atomic theory. He said that each element was made of its own kind of atom. Within an element, he said, all atoms were the same, but atoms of different elements had different sizes and masses.

Dalton did many experiments to find out how atoms of different elements react and combine. He weighed the starting materials and the combinations. He used wooden balls to build models of them. The balls represented different kinds of atoms with different weights.

Dalton's theory, his models, and his drawings of atoms helped other scientists. In fact, modern scientists use very similar models. Because Dalton's ideas were so useful to later scientists, he's often called the father of atomic theory.

In 1808, John Dalton wrote *A New System of Chemical Philosophy*. This book contained many of his ideas about atomic theory.

CHAPTER FOUR

ATOMIC SYMBOLS

Starting in 1803, Dalton invented symbols for the atoms of different elements he knew about. In time, he created 36 atomic symbols for elements including hydrogen and lead. He arranged them by their atomic mass. His symbol for hydrogen was a dot surrounded by a circle. His symbol for lead was an "L" in a circle.

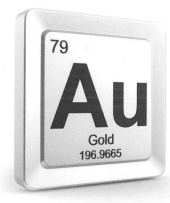

About 10 years later, chemist Jöns Jakob Berzelius created a simpler system, in which one or two letters each symbolized 47 elements. Many of those symbols are still used today. For example, "C" is carbon. "Au" is gold, for the Latin *aurum*.

In 1869, Russian chemist Dmitri Mendeleev changed things up again. He created a periodic table of 70 elements, all arranged by atomic weight. He even guessed about elements that hadn't been discovered yet and the properties of their atoms. However, this periodic table isn't quite the one we use today.

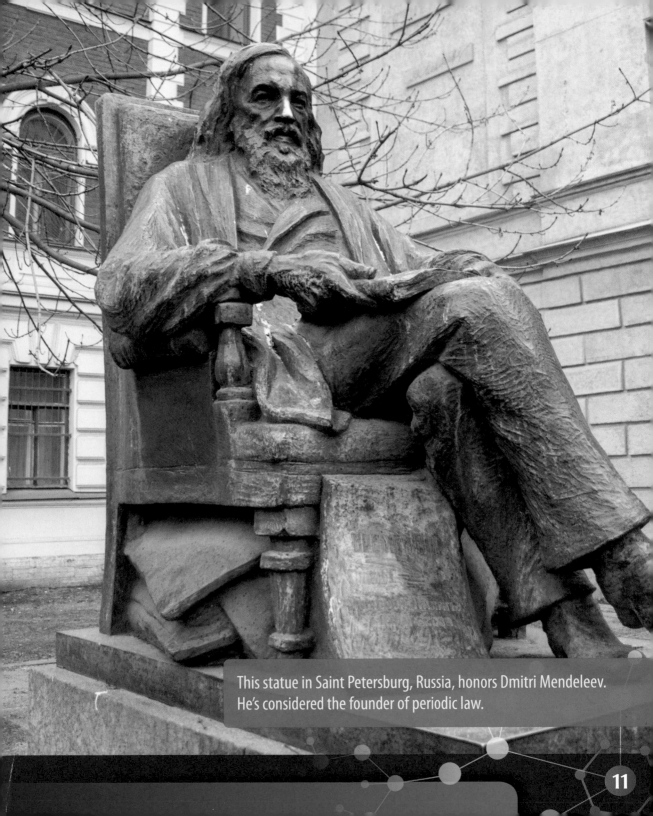

This statue in Saint Petersburg, Russia, honors Dmitri Mendeleev. He's considered the founder of periodic law.

CHAPTER FIVE

20TH CENTURY DISCOVERIES

For many years after Dalton, scientists thought that an atom was the smallest particle of matter. Then, in 1898, British scientist J. J. Thomson discovered electrons, tiny particles inside atoms. All atoms have electrons. Thomson called these very small particles "corpuscles." All the electrons together in an atom weigh less than 1/1,000 of the atom. They have a negative charge.

Each atom also has a nucleus, its center. Most of the mass of the atom is there. In 1911, scientist Ernest Rutherford discovered the existence of a nucleus in each atom. A nucleus is 100,000 times smaller than its atom. Most of an atom is empty space! The electrons surround the nucleus.

ERNEST RUTHERFORD

THOMSON
ATOMIC MODEL

RUTHERFORD
ATOMIC MODEL

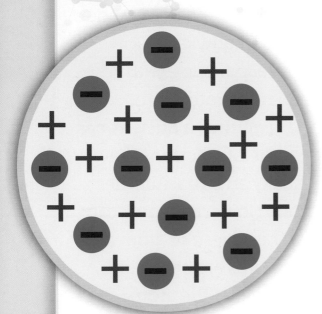

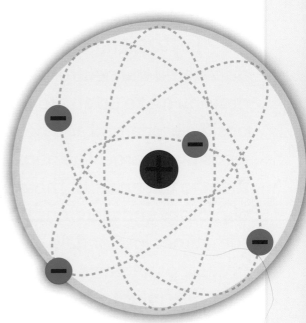

Thomson created what he called the "plum pudding" model of the atom. He thought the electrons were stuck through the atom like plums in a pudding. Rutherford, however, created the planetary model of the atom, in which electrons moved around the center like planets around the sun.

A nucleus itself is made up of particles called protons and neutrons. Rutherford discovered protons, too. These particles have a positive charge.

Danish scientist Niels Bohr worked with Rutherford. In 1913, Bohr created a more **accurate** atomic model. This model showed electrons orbiting the nucleus at certain energy levels. This newer model was called the Bohr model.

In 1928, English scientist James Chadwick discovered the neutron. These neutral particles, with protons, make up an atom's nucleus. As protons are positively charged and neutrons are neutral, a nucleus has a positive charge. The negative charge of electrons draws them to the nucleus. There are usually an equal number of protons and electrons in an atom. However, atoms can sometimes lose or gain electrons. This gives the atom a positive or negative charge. These atoms are called ions.

You might still see the Bohr model of the atom today, but now we know that electrons surround the nucleus in more of a cloud than a fixed pattern.

BOHR
ATOMIC MODEL

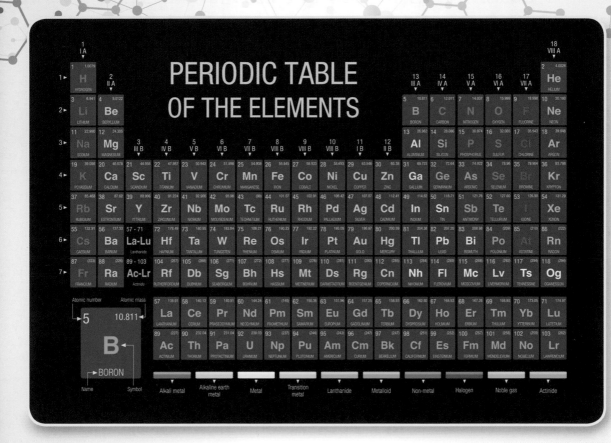

The number of protons in an atom's nucleus is its atomic number. Hydrogen, for example, has an atomic number of 1. Carbon has an atomic number of 6. Elements are arranged by atomic number on the periodic table we use today.

CHAPTER SIX

ATOMS THROUGH A MICROSCOPE

For many years, even the scientists who studied atoms hadn't actually seen one. Atoms are so small that, even with microscopes, people couldn't see them. However, in 1981, Swiss scientists Dr. Gerd Binnig and Dr. Heinrich Rohrer invented the scanning tunneling microscope. This invention was the foundation for scanning probe microscopy.

Scanning **probe** microscopes make images of surfaces by dragging a probe with a very sharp tip across the surface. The probe's point is so sharp that it may only be a single atom across at the tip. The probe tip travels over any bumps. Some of those bumps are individual atoms sticking up. A **laser** detects the height of the point. Then a computer shows an image of the bumps.

Scanning probe images are the closest we've come to seeing atoms. The images help scientists understand how atoms arrange themselves on surfaces.

Scanning tunneling microscopes can be used to study metal surfaces at the atomic level. They can even be used to study the surfaces of organic molecules such as DNA!

CHAPTER SEVEN

ATOMS IN LIVING THINGS

The green color of most plants comes from the **pigment** chlorophyll. Chlorophyll is a large molecule— two or more atoms joined together by chemical bonds—with one magnesium (Mg) atom at its center. These chemical bonds form when atoms from different elements take, give, or share electrons.

Magnesium doesn't account for much of a chlorophyll molecule, but it plays an important part. Without it, the plant can't use sunlight. This magnesium comes from the soil. If there's not enough magnesium in the soil, the green leaves turn white and the plant doesn't grow well. Farmers and gardeners can add magnesium to the soil to help their plants stay healthy.

Magnesium is an important element in the human body, too. Healthy **nerves**, muscles, and bones depend on it. We can get magnesium by eating green vegetables such as spinach and kale, bananas, and other things.

CHAPTER EIGHT

ATOMS AND MRIs

Doctors use X-rays to see bones in the body. However, X-rays don't show the body's soft tissues. Scientists in the 1950s knew that the nuclei of certain atoms—especially hydrogen atoms in water—respond to magnets. The soft tissues in our bodies contain a lot of water. It made sense to try to use that magnetic response to look inside the body. By the 1970s, researchers had built the first full-body magnetic resonance imaging (MRI) machine.

An MRI machine uses a very powerful magnet. The patient is placed inside the machine. Radio antennas detect the movement of hydrogen atoms in the soft tissues. Sometimes, to get a better image, a nurse or doctor will **inject** the patient with a special dye. An MRI helps doctors see how the body's working and if there's anything wrong. If they find something wrong, they'll use that information to treat the patient.

Radiologists are special doctors trained to examine MRI images and give a report to the doctor who ordered the MRI. They also oversee **technicians** as they perform MRI scans.

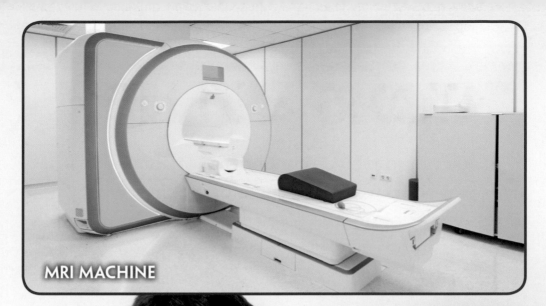

MRI MACHINE

CHAPTER NINE

COLORFUL LIGHTS

You've probably seen neon signs before. These signs may show words, numbers, or pictures. What makes it possible for these colorful signs to light up? Their glass tubes may contain neon, which is a **noble gas**. The glow is caused when the electricity strips electrons from the gas's atoms, which ionizes them, or turns them into ions. These ions are attracted to parts of the lamp and complete the electric circuit. The atoms in the lamp move around a lot and become excited, which means they gain a higher energy state. They release that energy as light.

Neon gas produces an orange-red color. Other noble gases can be used to make colorful signs, too. The colors depend on the orbits of the electrons in the gas atoms. Argon glows blue and is often mixed with other gases. Krypton glows a yellowish color.

Neon signs are all over the place. However, not all neon signs actually have neon gas in them!

CHAPTER TEN

ATOMIC CLOCKS

Have you heard of an atomic clock? The first accurate atomic clock was developed in the 1950s at the National Physical Laboratory in Great Britain. Atomic clocks are the most accurate timekeepers. Modern life depends on atomic clocks. Computer networks, cell phones, the power grid, and GPS **satellites** need exact timing.

FIRST CESIUM ATOMIC CLOCK, 1955

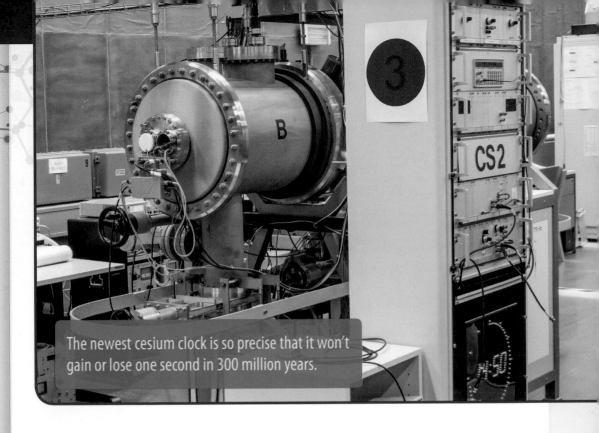

The newest cesium clock is so precise that it won't gain or lose one second in 300 million years.

How does an atomic clock work? That first clock started with an isotope of the element cesium. Isotopes are atoms that have the same atomic number but different mass numbers. This means they have different numbers of neutrons. Atoms of the isotope cesium-133, when they absorb or release energy, **resonate** at precisely the same frequency. It's so precise that it can be used to tell time very accurately! Scientists at many laboratories have been working to make atomic clocks more and more accurate over the years.

CHAPTER ELEVEN

DETECTING ATOMS

In the field of medicine, detecting small amounts of chemicals can be important. For example, even a small amount of lead in a child's blood can harm the growing brain. How do you detect five atoms out of a billion in a sample of blood? One way is with a spectroscope. It has three parts: a special light bulb, a gas burner, and a light detector, or photometer.

The blood sample is mixed with a gas and burned. Light from the bulb shines through the flame. The lead in the sample absorbs light. The detector measures the brightness of the light. If the light is dim, that means there's a lot of lead in the blood sample.

Other atoms can also be detected this way. Every kind of atom absorbs light of a different color. The spectroscope can see the colors from dozens of kinds of atoms.

This method, called atomic absorption spectroscopy (AAS), is only used to tell if there are metals present in a sample.

CHAPTER TWELVE

THE CUTTING EDGE

Starting in 1911, an adventurous Austrian physicist named Victor Hess made 10 balloon flights. He discovered that particles called cosmic rays rain down on Earth's atmosphere from space. The cosmic rays move so fast that when they hit other particles in the atmosphere, they can split atoms. Scientists learned that atoms weren't the smallest particles of matter after all!

Starting in the 1950s, scientists built machines to study this process. These machines are called particle accelerators. They crash nuclei and electrons into targets. Because they break atoms into smaller pieces, scientists nicknamed them atom smashers. By looking at what's inside nuclei, scientists are finding out the stuff that all matter is made of. Thousands of particle accelerators are now in use. The largest ones smash heavy nuclei such as those of the element lead. Smaller accelerators help detect and treat illness.

Fermilab in Batavia, Illinois, is a particle physics and accelerator laboratory. PIP-II is a 705.4-foot-(215 m) long linear particle accelerator there.

CHAPTER THIRTEEN

THINK LIKE A CHEMIST

If you were born in ancient Greece, you would think that the world was made up of earth, air, fire, and water. If you were born in the 1600s, you'd think there were only a few kinds of atoms. We now know there are 94 naturally occurring elements on Earth. Clever chemists are always finding new ways to combine them. So far, there are over 140 million combinations! Some of the new combinations are medicines. Some are plastics. Others may make cell phones better and faster.

Now that you know about atoms, you can think like a chemist. Take a deep breath. Imagine the atoms of oxygen going into your lungs. Step in a puddle. Think about the hydrogen and oxygen atoms that make up the water. Look around. Remember that everything is made of atoms, and atoms matter!

GLOSSARY

accurate (AA-kyuh-ruht) Free of mistakes.

chemist (KEH-mist) Someone trained in chemistry, a science that deals with the structure and properties of substances and their changes.

inject (ihn-JEHKT) To force something into the body using a needle or sharp teeth.

laser (LAY-zuhr) A device that produces a narrow beam of light.

nerve (NUHRV) One of the many thin parts that control movement and feeling by carrying messages between the brain and other parts of the body.

noble gas (NOH-buhl GAAS) Any of a group of rare gases that exhibit great stability and extremely low reaction rates.

philosopher (fuh-LAH-suh-fuhr) A person who tries to discover and to understand the basic nature of knowledge.

pigment (PIHG-muhnt) A substance that gives color to something else.

probe (PROHB) A long, thin instrument that is used especially for examining parts of the body.

resonate (REH-zuh-nayt) To produce a vibration.

satellite (SAA-tuh-lyt) A spacecraft placed in orbit around Earth, a moon, or a planet to collect information or for communication.

technician (tek-NIH-shuhn) A person skilled in the details or techniques of a subject, art, or job.

INDEX

PRIMARY SOURCE LIST

Page 7
Robert Boyle and Denis Papin. Wood engraving. 1870. Now kept by Universal Images Group/
Getty Images.

Page 9
Frontispiece of *John Dalton and the Rise of Modern Chemistry* by Henry Roscoe. Engraving of a
painting. William Henry Worthington (engraver) and Joseph Allen (painter). 1895. Now kept
by Wikimedia Commons.

Page 17
The first scanning tunneling microscope. Photograph. 1986. Now kept by SSPL/Getty Images.

WEBSITES

Due to the changing nature of Internet links, PowerKids Press has developed an online list
of websites related to the subject of this book. This site is updated regularly. Please use
this link to access the list: www.powerkidslinks.com/sops/atoms